Still a Babe after all these Years?

Take this Birthday Quiz to find out.

FLIP THE PAGES FOR ADDED FUN!

ILLUSTRATED BY: Ken O'Brien

At your age, it's important to keep attending aerobics classes because:

(A)

THE HEALTHIER YOU ARE, THE MORE ENERGY YOU'LL HAVE.

(B)

THE MORE YOU EXERCISE, THE THINNER YOU'LL BE.

(C)

THE MORE ATTRACTIVE, WELL-TONED WOMEN YOU CAN "ACCIDENTALLY" FALL ON AND PUT OUT OF COMMISSION FOR A WHILE, THE BETTER.

Match the following foods and where they will eventually end up.

A. BIRTHDAY CAKE

B. BROWNIES

C. PREMIUM ICE CREAM

D. CARROT STICKS

_ YOUR HIPS

_ YOUR THIGHS

_ YOUR BUTT

_ THE GARBAGE DISPOSAL

Two women your age, one heading north and the other heading west, arrive at a 4-way stop sign at exactly the same moment. Which woman has the right of way?

ANSWER: WHICHEVER ONE IS THE LATEST FOR HER WEEKLY HAIRSTYLING AND DYE JOB.

multiple CHOICE

When the temperature gets warmer, it's especially important for women your age to:

(A) INCREASE THEIR WATER INTAKE.

(B) DECREASE ACTIVITY LEVEL WHILE OUTDOORS.

(C) SIT DOWN! YOU'RE HAVING ANOTHER HOT FLASH!

What do you see in this picture?

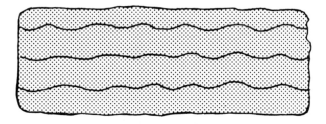

Ⓐ A FOUR-LAYER BIRTHDAY CAKE.

Ⓑ A LAKE ON A WINDY DAY.

Ⓒ YOUR FOREHEAD IN A REARVIEW MIRROR.

MATCHING

Match the attributes of men on the left with their marital status on the RIGHT.

Ⓐ GOOD-LOOKING.

Ⓑ CHARMING.

Ⓒ SEXY.

Ⓓ DROP-DEAD GORGEOUS.

_ MARRIED.

_ HAPPILY MARRIED.

_ MARRIED WITH KIDS.

_ JUST MARRIED.

which gray hair is longer?

_____

_____

ANSWER: THEY'RE BOTH THE SAME, AS YOU CAN CLEARLY SEE WHEN YOU YANK THEM OUT.

Multiple Choice

Some men no longer find women your age attractive because:

(A) THEY NEED TO PROVE THEIR VIRILITY BY DATING YOUNGER WOMEN.

(B) LOOKING AT YOU WOULD BE A REMINDER TO THEIR FRAGILE EGOS THAT THEY ARE NO LONGER SPRING CHICKENS.

(C) THEY STILL HAVE THEIR EYESIGHT.

What do you see when you connect the dots in the order they're numbered?

.1

.2

ANSWER: THE DIRECTION YOUR BOOBS WILL BE HEADING FROM NOW ON.

MULTIPLE CHOICE

when you see the movie "LOVE STORY," you still cry because:

(A) YOU DON'T LOSE YOUR ROMANTIC NATURE WITH AGE.

(B) IT REMINDS YOU OF THE SAD FACT OF HUMAN MORTALITY.

(C) YOU'LL NEVER AGAIN BE AS THIN AS THAT ACTRESS WHO STARRED IN IT.

(1) You go out to dinner on your birthday. You order the salad bar, skip the high-fat dressings, ignore the bacon bits, use artificial sweetener in your iced tea, and avoid crackers or bread. How much weight will you gain?

ANSWER: WELL, COUNTING THE TRIPLE HOT-FUDGE SUNDAE YOU'LL ORDER FOR DESSERT, ABOUT A TON.

13

MULTIPLE CHOICE

If a woman your age were to appear on that TV show that arranges dates, she would most likely be chosen because of her:

A SENSUALLY VOLUPTUOUS VOICE.

B QUICK, WITTY ANSWERS.

C IMPLIED WILLINGNESS TO DO JUST ABOUT ANYTHING WITH A STRANGER IF IT MEANT A TRIP TO HAWAII.

MATCHING

Following are some effective hair treatments for a woman your age. Match the cost to the hair treatment.

Ⓐ PERM Ⓑ FROST Ⓒ DYE Ⓓ BAG OVER HEAD

___ $70
___ $45
___ FREE
___ $60

It's a good bet your lover still gets:

Ⓐ
TO PAY THE
DINNER BILL.

Ⓑ
ROMANTIC
AT EVERY
OPPORTUNITY.

Ⓒ
THE WILLIES
SEEING YOU
NAKED.

"FORD"

is the name of _____.

ANSWER: THE PRESIDENT WHO WAS IN OFFICE LAST TIME YOU HAD SEX.

Unscramble the letters to reveal the name of anyone who looks better in spandex than you.

What do you see in this picture?

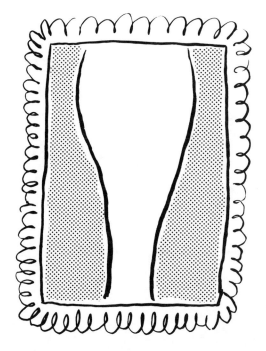

A) AN ANCIENT MIDDLE-EASTERN VASE.

B) THE METAL PART OF A LAMP WHERE THE BULB GOES.

C) YOUR UPPER ARM IN A SLEEVELESS BLOUSE.

You're willing to date a younger guy because:

Ⓐ YOU'RE OPEN-MINDED ENOUGH TO CONSIDER ALL OPTIONS.

Ⓑ YOU REFUSE TO CATEGORIZE SOMEONE BECAUSE OF HIS YOUTH.

Ⓒ AT YOUR AGE, THEY'RE ALL YOUNGER GUYS.

(oops... Sorry.   It just occurred to us that a woman your age might not remember what the word "Multiple" means.)

MULTIPLE CHOICE

Where are you most likely to see a younger man on the arm of a woman your age?

Ⓐ AT THE BALLET.

Ⓑ AT A FANCY RESTAURANT.

Ⓒ IN A CROSSWALK.

Q. which is warmest:

the beach, the desert or the jungle?

A. WHICHEVER PLACE YOU ARE WHEN YOU HAVE ANOTHER HOT FLASH.

Cute guys still whistle at women your age.

TRUE! BUT ONLY IF WOMEN YOUR AGE ARE DRIVING CABS.

MULTIPLE CHOICE
what do you think of when you hear the word "ZIP"?
A
WHAT YOU HAVE TO LIE DOWN TO DO TO YOUR JEANS.
B
THE NOISE TIME MAKES AS IT SPEEDS BY.
C
YOUR CHANCES OF EVER BEING PROMOTED AS LONG AS THE "OLD BOY NETWORK" IS IN PLACE.
27

WHICH IS APPROPRIATE?

Choose the appropriate vanity plate for the car of a person your age.

when a woman your age eats two
bowls of ice cream, it means she's...

Ⓐ

Ⓑ

Ⓒ

HUNGRY.

DEPRESSED.

CUTTING
BACK.

29

Reading Comprehension

Susan gets home from a long day at work, changes out of her work clothes, and starts to make dinner. She has to stop because the recipe calls for milk, and there's none left. While she is at the store, her husband comes home, removes his tie, and leaves to get the mail. When he returns, Susan has resumed cooking dinner, so he reads the paper.

what is the theme of this paragraph?

ANSWER: HE ALWAYS, ALWAYS USES ALL THE STUPID MILK WITHOUT TELLING HER! CAN'T HE, JUST ONCE, GO TO THE STUPID STORE AND GET MORE STUPID MILK HIMSELF? WOULD IT KILL HIM?

there are several anti-aging creams that really work.

FALSE! BUT YOU'LL CONTINUE TO BUY THEM BY THE TRUCKLOAD ANYWAY.

When swimsuit season comes around, you should choose:

Ⓐ
A SENSIBLE ONE-PIECE.

Ⓑ
A SLIGHTLY MORE DARING TWO-PIECE.

Ⓒ
A HIDING PLACE.

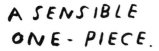

33

Maze

Find the path that leads you through the maze to Mr. Right.

YOU

MR. RIGHT

SOLUTION: TRICK MAZE! NO MATTER WHICH WAY YOU GO, BY THE TIME YOU GET TO MR. RIGHT, HE'LL BE MARRIED!

If you have one quarter, one dime, a half-dollar and a penny, how much change do you have?

ANSWER: CHANGE!? CHANGE!? WHAT D'YA MEAN, CHANGE!? IS THAT SOME KIND OF WISECRACK!?

Beauty comes from inside.

TRUE! INSIDE THE MAKE-UP BAG,
INSIDE THE COLD CREAM JAR, INSIDE
THE MOISTURIZER TUBE...

multiple choice

What would be the very worst disaster you could imagine?

(A)

THE EARTH IS INVADED BY CREATURES FROM ANOTHER GALAXY WHO ENSLAVE US ALL.

(B)

THE SUN BURNS OUT, CASTING THE WORLD INTO FREEZING DARKNESS.

(C)

HOT PANTS COME BACK INTO FASHION.

Optical illusion

Which waistband is bigger?

Ⓐ

Ⓑ

ANSWER: B. IT'S ELASTIC, JUST LIKE ALL THE WAISTBANDS ON ALL THE PANTS YOU'LL BE BUYING FROM NOW ON.

Men age better than Women.

FALSE! WHEN'S THE LAST TIME YOU SAW A
WOMAN COMB ALL HER HAIR OVER TO
ONE SIDE TO COVER A BALD SPOT?

What do you get when you connect the dots in the correct sequence?

.1

.2

ANSWER: YOU GET A HEADACHE. YOU FORGOT TO PUT ON YOUR READING GLASSES FIRST.

The dance you're most likely to be doing on your birthday is:

Ⓐ
THE CHA-CHA.

Ⓑ
THE ACHY-BREAKY.

Ⓒ
THAT DANCE YOU DO BACK AND FORTH ON ONE FOOT WHILE YOU WAIT FOR THE BATHROOM.

Women your age always need more clothes.

TRUE! THE MORE CLOTHES YOU WEAR, THE BETTER.

What's wrong with this picture?

Ⓐ SHE'S LIFTING WITH HER BACK INSTEAD OF HER SHOULDERS.

Ⓑ HER HANDS SHOULD BE FURTHER APART ON THE BAR.

Ⓒ SHE'S WEARING SPANDEX IN PUBLIC.

When men see you in blue Jeans, their first thought probably is:

Ⓐ "MAN! SHE LOOKS GREAT!"

Ⓑ "GEE! I'D LIKE TO MEET HER!"

Ⓒ "WOW! THAT DENIM IS REALLY STRONG!"

47

Beauty is in the eye of the beholder.

TRUE! BUT BEHOLDERS YOUR AGE ARE TOUGH TO FIND.

Which doesn't belong?

ANSWER: TRICK QUESTION! THEY ALL BELONG, BECAUSE YOU OWN THEM!

When you hear the term "fast food," you think of:

Ⓐ
A DRIVE-THROUGH HAMBURGER RESTAURANT.

Ⓑ
A MICROWAVE MEAL.

Ⓒ
THE THIRD PIECE OF CAKE YOU WOLFED DOWN WHILE YOU THOUGHT NO ONE WAS LOOKING.

Unscramble the words below to find an activity popular with women your age.

POLYESTER   CLOTHING

SHOPPING   FOR

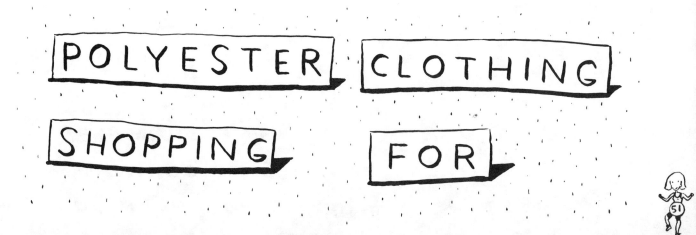

With age comes _____.

ANSWER: SCARY LITTLE DIMPLES ON
YOUR THIGHS THAT DON'T GO AWAY NO
MATTER HOW OFTEN YOU WORK OUT.

What is an appropriate birthday activity for a woman your age?

Riddle

Why did the woman your age cross the road?

ANSWER: BECAUSE SHE SAW A WOMAN APPROACHING WHOM SHE HADN'T SEEN IN A LONG, LONG TIME WHO HADN'T CHANGED A BIT.

Match the item to the location where it can be found.

Ⓐ
YOUR CHILDHOOD LUNCHBOX.

Ⓑ
YOUR FIRST HAIR DRYER.

Ⓒ
YOUR FAVORITE ICE SKATES.

Ⓓ
YOUR PROM DRESS.

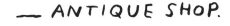

___ ANTIQUE SHOP.

___ ANTIQUE SHOP.

___ ANTIQUE SHOP.

___ ANTIQUE SHOP.

what is it?

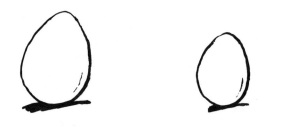

A AN OSTRICH EGG NEXT TO A CHICKEN EGG.

B A CHICKEN EGG NEXT TO A ROBIN EGG.

C YOUR PANTYHOSE EGG NEXT TO A REGULAR SIZE PANTYHOSE EGG.

Maze

Try to find your way through the torturous visual acuity test designed specifically for the eyesight of a woman your age.

START   FINISH

STORY PROBLEM

Sally and Betty decide to celebrate Sally's birthday with a trip to the neighborhood mall. If Sally starts with $50°°, and Betty starts with $40°°, and Sally buys a blouse for $30°° and shoes for $20°°, and Betty purchases a 40°° hat, how much money do they have left?

ANSWER: WHO CARES? THAT'S WHY THEY HAVE CHARGE CARDS.

If you had a talking scale, it would probably say:

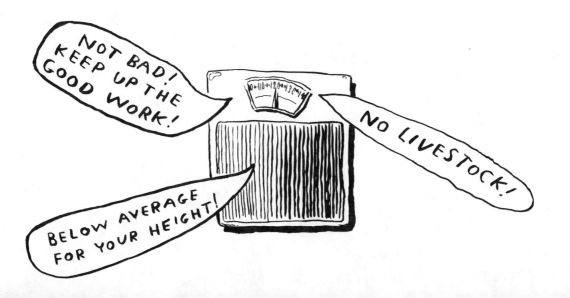

Riddle

Why did the woman your age sit on the fence?

ANSWER: WHEN SHE REMARKED THAT SHE "JUST COULDN'T SEEM TO GAIN WEIGHT," THE OTHER WOMEN GANGED UP ON HER AND CHASED HER OUT OF THE HOUSE.

What do you see?

Ⓐ
A GROUP OF
SLEEPING
SNAKES.

Ⓑ
HEAT RISING
OFF A PAVEMENT.

Ⓒ
GRAY HAIRS
YOU PLUCKED
SINCE THIS
MORNING.

Multiple Choice
What are men usually looking for in a woman your age?
(A) COMPANIONSHIP.
(B) SHARED INTERESTS.
ME TOO
ME TOO
(C) A YOUNGER SISTER.
62

You can still wear the clothes you wore in college.

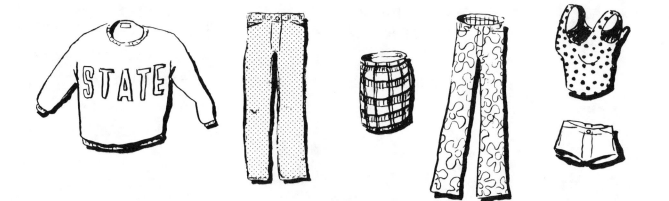

TRUE! OR YOU CAN BREATHE, YOUR CHOICE!

63

Multiple Choice

The worst moment for a woman is when she:

A
FINDS HER FIRST GRAY HAIR.

B
NOTICES WRINKLES ON HER BROW.

C
SEES A SNAPSHOT OF HERSELF AND SAYS, "HEY! HOW COME MOM'S WEARING MY CLOTHES?"

When you hear the word "farm," what is the first thing that pops into your head?

Ⓐ OLD MACDONALD.   Ⓑ LIVESTOCK.   Ⓒ FAT.

After work, Lisa stops at the supermarket to buy a few last-minute items for her birthday dinner. When her purchases have been sacked, the young man asks if she'd like help taking the bags to the car. Lisa shakes her head and thanks him. In response, he smiles and says, "Have a nice evening. Ma'am."

The theme of this paragraph is:

Ⓐ

STORES ARE REALLY GOING OUT OF THEIR WAY TO PLEASE CUSTOMERS.

Ⓑ

SACKERS GROW MORE POLITE AND CONSIDERATE ALL THE TIME.

Ⓒ

"MA'AM! HE CALLED ME MA'AM! WHO DOES HE THINK I AM... HIS MOTHER?"

GROCERY

Help the woman your age find the appropriate store.

Matching

Match the conditions experienced by your birthday party guests at left with the appropriate response at right.

Ⓐ GUEST HAS GAINED WEIGHT.

Ⓑ GUEST IS DATING LOSER.

Ⓒ GUEST IS WEARING BAD OUTFIT.

Ⓓ GUEST HAS DYED HER HAIR.

— GOSSIP ABOUT HER.

— GOSSIP ABOUT HER.

— GOSSIP ABOUT HER.

— GOSSIP ABOUT HER.

WRITTEN BY:

chris Brethwaite, Bill Bridgeman, Bill Gray, Allyson Jones, Kevin Kinzer, Mark Oatman, Dee Ann Stewart, Dan Taylor, Rich Warwick and Myra Zirkle.

Books from:

SHOEBOX GREETINGS

(A tiny little division of Hallmark)

STILL MARRIED AFTER ALL THESE YEARS

DON'T WORRY, BE CRABBY: Maxine's Guide to Life

40: THE YEAR OF NAPPING DANGEROUSLY

THE MOM DICTIONARY

THE DAD DICTIONARY

WORKIN' NOON TO FIVE: The Official Workplace Quiz Book

WHAT... ME, 30?

THE FISHING DICTIONARY

YOU EXPECT ME TO SWALLOW THAT? The Official Hospital Quiz Book

THE GOOD, THE PLAID AND THE BOGEY: A Glossary of Golfing Terms

THE CHINA PATTERN SYNDROME: Your Wedding and How to Survive It

THE GRANDPARENT DICTIONARY

STILL A BABE AFTER ALL THESE YEARS?

CRABBY ROAD: More Thoughts on Life From Maxine

THE HANDYMAN DICTIONARY A Guide For the Home Mess-It-Up-Yourselfer